God's Word and Jesus

Think

Ask

Bible

Dedication
For Howard and Julia Martin
Whose love for Jesus has graced their family,
making them a blessing to their children and
grandchildren. With grateful thanks for your support,
encouragement and love.

Lx

God's Word and Jesus

What the Bible Teaches about The Gospel,
Evangelism, Prayer and other Essential Stuff

Laura Martin

CF4•K

Copyright © Laura Martin 2017

10 9 8 7 6 5 4 3 2 1

Paperback ISBN: 978-1-5271-0047-3

e-pub ISBN: 978-1-5271-0079-4

mobi ISBN: 978-1-5271-0080-0

First published in 2017 by

Christian Focus Publications Ltd,

Geanies House, Fearn, Ross-shire

IV20 1TW, Scotland

www.christianfocus.com

Cover and internal page design by Pete Barnsley (Creativehoot.com)

Printed and bound by Bell and Bain, Glasgow

Scripture quotations are from The ESV®Bible (The Holy Bible, English Standard
Version®), published by HarperCollinsPublishers, ©2001 by Crossway. Used by
permission. All rights reserved.

CONTENTS

What does the Bible say about...?

What does the
Bible say about...

The Gospel?

Think

Ask

Bible

There was once a Pharisee whose soul was troubled. In Bible times a Pharisee was a Jewish man and a religious leader. Pharisees prided themselves as being 'law keepers'. Not only did they keep all the Old Testament laws, they would even make up more laws (really crazy ones) to show how righteous and good they were.

Did You Know ...?

The Pharisees were determined to 'Keep the Sabbath holy' by not working on that day. So they actually made a law saying how many steps you were allowed to walk before it was considered work!

Pharisees were proud of their position in society and often drew attention to themselves to show how 'holy' they were. Or at least, they thought they were, but they were wrong. When God gave the law to Moses in the Old Testament, He knew it would be impossible for people to obey it all of the time. Why? Because the law addresses issues of the heart, and the heart of every man, woman and child is sinful. Remember when Adam and Eve first sinned back in the garden of Eden? Well, that changed everything for every person born since. It meant that every child born from that point on was born a sinner. Do you think that is unfair? Because Adam and Eve made a terrible mistake, we are all born sinners! But it's not unfair. In fact it's the opposite. Sin deserves punishment yet God has provided a rescue plan for us. Keep reading.....

> [12]*Therefore, just as sin came into the world through one man, and death through sin, and so death spread to all men because all sinned. (Romans 5:12)*

Back to the troubled Pharisee. What was going on with him? Well the problem started when he heard some teachings which unsettled Him. Teachings about sin, repentance and salvation.

Sin is any actions, thoughts, attitudes and behaviours which are dishonouring to God. Repentance is when we agree with God, that we are sinful, and we turn away from our sin and ask His forgiveness. In fact, the word 'repent' actually means to 'change your mind'. You could picture repentance as turning 180 degrees from the direction you were heading. For example, if we were back-chatting parents or teachers, to repent (or change your mind) means to turn and go in the opposite direction, making sure our responses are respectful.

But the Pharisees didn't understand any of this. They thought that doing right things outwardly (like following a bunch of rules) was enough to get them to heaven. But it wasn't. So, this Pharisee, whose name was Nicodemus, was troubled because he didn't know how to respond to all of this strange teaching he had heard. However he did know one thing he could do. He waited until it was dark and then he left his house and went to the One who could help him. He went to Jesus. Why did Nicodemus visit Jesus at night under the cover of darkness? It was because the Pharisees were a prideful bunch. They believed they were the ones with the answers. Nicodemus didn't want anyone else to know his soul was troubled, but he knew that he needed to go to Jesus. He knew he needed to know the truth about eternal life. Nicodemus did exactly the right thing. God had sent Jesus, His beloved Son to bring the good news of forgiveness and salvation to all who would believe in Him.

> [1] Now there was a man of the Pharisees named Nicodemus, a ruler of the Jews. [2] This man came to Jesus by night and said to him, "Rabbi, we know that you are a teacher come from God, for no one can do these signs that you do unless God is with him." [3] Jesus answered him, "Truly, truly, I say to you, unless one is born again he cannot see the kingdom of God." [4] Nicodemus said to him, "How can a man be born when he

> is old? Can he enter a second time into his mother's womb
> and be born?" ⁵ Jesus answered, "Truly, truly, I say to you,
> unless one is born of water and the Spirit, he cannot enter the
> kingdom of God. ⁶ That which is born of the flesh is flesh, and
> that which is born of the Spirit is spirit." (John 3:1-8)

Jesus told Nicodemus what he needed to know, He told him that those who are born again will have eternal life. Notice that Jesus didn't say anything about following rules. Of course, the idea of being born again was very strange to Nicodemus. The only 'birth' he knew of was when a baby was born. He wondered how that could happen to someone who has already been born once before. However, Jesus wasn't meaning that you had to literally be born again. He was meaning that there needed to be new life. So, He answered Nicodemus again.

> ⁵Jesus answered, "Truly, truly, I say to you, unless one is born
> of water and the Spirit, he cannot enter the kingdom of God."
> (John 3:5)

When Jesus speaks of being born of water and Spirit, He means this: the water represents cleansing of sin. The Spirit of God is the one who gives new and transformed life into a person's cleansed (forgiven) heart.

Jesus was saying that the heart of a person is sinful and needs cleansing and transforming. It can't be done by good works or even by following a long list of rules. It can only be done by the work of God to cleanse us and forgive us our sins and transform us to be more like Him.

But why must this cleansing and transforming work be done? Can't God love us just as we are and accept us into heaven without us having to change? Well, God does love us as we are. Very much in fact. But God is a holy God. He is perfect and righteous and good, and He cannot be in the presence of sin. That means He cannot accept us as we are, as sinners. It's not our personalities or our looks that need to change. We don't need to be funnier, or more creative, or cooler. No, God made us all unique and wonderful, right down to the freckles on our noses and our loud laughs! It's the sin in us that is the problem. That is what needs to be dealt with. But we can't deal with it. You might remember the Bible speaks of people making sacrifices of animals to pay for their sin.

> *23For the wages of sin is death, but the free gift of God is eternal life in Christ Jesus our Lord. (Romans 6:23)*

The consequence (or the wages) of sin, is death. But when Jesus came, He died on our behalf to pay for the sin of all who would believe in Him. Isn't that amazing? Jesus put it this way when He was explaining to Nicodemus this very same thing.

> *16"For God so loved the world, that he gave his only Son, that whoever believes in Him should not perish but have eternal life." (John 3:16)*

Remember, I said that the Pharisees didn't understand what salvation was? Salvation means 'being saved', and the Pharisees didn't see their need to be saved. They did not understand that they were sinners, just as you and I are, and that continuing to live a life in sin would mean that they would face death. The word 'death' does of course mean 'physical death', but in this case it means something much more significant. It means eternal separation from God. The sad thing about the Pharisees is that they had Jesus right there with them, telling them the truth about life and death and sin and forgiveness. However, they did not want to know. They wanted to keep their sin and their position of power over people. The sad thing today, is that many people are just like the Pharisees. People do not want to know that they are sinners because they love their sin and do not want to give it up. They do not understand that the consequences of their unforgiven sin will mean not only physical death but eternal separation from God. Nicodemus, however, was different. He knew that he was in trouble. He knew that he needed to be saved from his sin, but he didn't know how. So, Jesus told him. Did Nicodemus believe Jesus? Perhaps not straight away but at some time Nicodemus repented of his sin and believed in Jesus as his Saviour. In fact, after Jesus was crucified, Nicodemus was one of the men who came forward to take Jesus' body and prepare it for burial in the tomb. Imagine that! The Pharisees wanted Jesus dead and they succeeded, but one of their own kind had experienced the life transforming forgiveness of Jesus, and served Jesus as best he could, by taking His body to prepare it for burial. What must the other Pharisees have thought? Nicodemus didn't care. He had been saved from his sin and born again into a new life with Jesus as his Lord and Saviour. Nicodemus loved Jesus because Jesus loved Nicodemus. How about you. Do you love Jesus?

But Wait there's More!

What other Principles can we Learn from Scripture?

What is the gospel? It is the good news that first tells us that we are all sinners and that our sin separates us from God, who is Holy and cannot be in the presence of sin. That might not seem like good news to you – but it doesn't end there. God, who loves the world so much, sent His Son Jesus to come to this earth and live, and to die a horrible death on the cross as the sacrifice and payment for sin on our behalf. To be saved we must turn from our sin, asking God's forgiveness, accept Jesus as our Saviour, trusting and believing in Him, God's Son

▼ more...

who provides eternal life through His death and resurrection. Then, with His help, we follow Jesus all our days.

That is amazing to me. That God would love us so much that He would provide us with a rescue plan, to rescue us from the penalty of our sin and provide us a way, through His Son Jesus, to be forgiven and part of His forever family.

The gospel is the most beautiful gift in the whole world! Let me highlight just three things about the gospel I find so overwhelming.

- **GRACE**

Grace is a common name for girls and in fact my eldest daughter has Grace as her middle name. It means 'unmerited or undeserved favour'. Or more simply put, 'a gift we don't deserve'. That's what babies are to mums and dads – precious gifts that we don't deserve. But the Bible uses the word 'grace' in a more specific way. The Bible uses it to describe favour from God that we don't deserve.

> [8] For by grace you have been saved through faith. And this is not your own doing; it is the gift of God, [9] not a result of works, so that no one may boast. [10] For we are His workmanship, created in Christ Jesus for good works, which God prepared beforehand, that we should walk in them. (Ephesians 2:8-10)

The Gospel is one example of God's grace to us. God's rescue plan for sinners, even though none of us deserve it. Salvation is something that only God can give us, because Jesus' death on the cross paid for our sin. There is nothing we can do to earn salvation. In fact, verse 10 reminds us that whatever good work a Christian does, it's only because God enables them to be good at it. Not only can we not

▼ *more...*

save ourselves, we can't even boast about things we are good at because God gave us those abilities anyway. So, it really is only by God's grace that we can be saved, through faith in Jesus. Isn't that awesome? Even though we have sinned against God, God provided the way for us to return to Him. Wow. That's what grace is. God's gift to us, that we really don't deserve. I am so thankful for it! Are you?

- **MERCY**

Mercy is a word which describes showing compassion or kindness towards someone who doesn't deserve it. God, in the Gospel, has shown us the greatest mercy that anyone could ask for. Read this next account which is a picture of the mercy that God has shown us.

> [23] "Therefore the kingdom of heaven may be compared to a king who wished to settle accounts with his servants. [24] When he began to settle, one was brought to him who owed him ten thousand talents. [25] And since he could not pay, his master ordered him to be sold, with his wife and children and all that he had, and payment to be made. [26] So the servant fell on his knees, imploring him, 'Have patience with me, and I will pay you everything.' [27] And out of pity for him, the master of that servant released him and forgave him the debt."
> (Matthew 18:23-27)

The master in the parable represents God. He called his servants to account, wanting back all that they owed him. Remember, we all owe God a debt because of our sin. It seemed that this one servant owed a debt that he could not pay back, but he cried out to his master for mercy. Of course, he would never be able to pay back that debt.

▼ more...

9

One talent was worth about sixteen years of wages. The servant owed 10,000 talents. Have you worked that out? It's about 160,000 years of wages. Obviously, it was a far greater debt than what the servant would ever be able to repay. It seems hopeless doesn't it? But here is where it gets pretty neat. The master forgives the man his debt. Completely. The master didn't do what his servant asked, remember the servant wanted time to pay back the debt (uh – how was he planning on doing that?) Nope, the master shows great mercy and took on the debt himself and released the servant from it. You have probably guessed that the master in the parable represents God, and the servant represents us. We have such a huge debt with God because of our sin and we will never ever be able to pay for it. But God, who is rich in mercy, hears us when we cry out to Him for forgiveness, and He freely gives it. Our debt, just like the servant's debt, is wiped completely. Wow. I have to ask, have you cried out to God for His mercy, to forgive you from the debt of your sin?

- **ETERNAL LIFE**

When God first made man to live in the garden with Him, it was to be their forever home. But sadly, the man and woman, Adam and Eve, chose otherwise. They chose independence from God by choosing to sin, and so they had to leave God's Holy presence. Because of their sin the perfect environment changed to a cursed one. Remember, the Garden of Eden was God's garden. It was where He walked in the cool of the evening with Adam and Eve. There were animals of every kind all living in perfect harmony. There was food freely available to meet every need. It was breathtakingly beautiful. And there was no death - none, not even of the animals. Then came that first sin. Think

▼ *more...*

about what that meant. What a beautiful life they could have lived! But they chose sin. Not only did Adam and Eve have to leave God's presence in the garden but they were separated from God. When God made man and woman, He made them to live forever. When sin entered the world, part of the curse of sin was that the body began to decay and fail, which ultimately leads to physical death. But the soul of a person lives on. That's the part that is 'you' – your personality, your thoughts and emotions. That part of a human will live forever. You can see the problem, can't you? If a person is separated from God because of their sin, what happens to their soul when they die?

> [16]*"For God so loved the world that he gave his only Son, that whoever believes in him should not perish but have eternal life." (John 3:16)*

To 'perish' means that those people who don't believe in God as their Saviour, will go to a place without God for all eternity. The Bible describes it as a place of destruction, a place of weeping and gnashing of teeth. You perhaps have heard that this place is called hell.

But those who do believe in the Lord Jesus as their Lord and Saviour, receive eternal life and will enter heaven with God, and with everyone else who has been saved from their sin. What wonderful reunions there will be for those who have passed away before us – and how lovely to think that all who are saved from their sin, through the death of Jesus on the cross, get to spend all eternity together, worshipping God together!

What did we Learn about the Gospel?

Ask

- God made man (men, women and children) to be in relationship with Him, but when man chose sin, that broke the relationship, because God is a Holy God who cannot be in the presence of sin.

- All men, women and children are born sinners and all need a saviour.

- God sent His only Son Jesus, to die on the cross to pay the penalty for our sin.

- Forgiveness from sin is available to all who acknowledge their sin before God, understanding that there is nothing that they can do to earn forgiveness or God's favour, but instead receive His forgiveness as a gift of grace.

- When someone is saved from their sin, they are said to be 'born again' – they are dead to their old life of sin, and alive in their new life with Jesus as their Lord.

- God shows us grace – His undeserved favour towards us.

- God shows us mercy – complete kindness to free us from the debt of sin.

- God gives eternal life and one day a home with Him in heaven, and that is only available through repenting of sin and believing in the Lord Jesus Christ as our Saviour.

Study Questions

Think

[16] "For God so loved the world, that he gave his only Son, that whoever believes in him should not perish but have eternal life. [17] For God did not send his Son into the world to condemn the world, but in order that the world might be saved through him. [18] Whoever believes in him is not condemned, but whoever does not believe is condemned already, because he has not believed in the name of the only Son of God. [19] And this is the judgment: the light has come into the world, and people loved the darkness rather than the light because their works were evil. [20] For everyone who does wicked things hates the light and does not come to the light, lest his works should be exposed. (John 3:16-20)

1. Look at the word 'world' in the above scriptures. Read the sentence again. Does it mean the world, as in the creation around us that we love to enjoy? Or does it mean the peoples of the world?

2. Is the gospel (the good news) of salvation available to everyone, or is it only for a certain group of people? (Use the above verses to answer)

3. Verse 16 tells us that there are two options for people. What are they?

4. Using the above scriptures, answer how people can avoid perishing but instead have eternal life.

5. Why did God send His Son Jesus into the world?

6. The word 'condemned' (v.18) means 'to receive a sentence of punishment'. What two qualities of God have you learnt about today that led Him to provide salvation from condemnation?

▼ more...

7. According to verse 18, who is condemned?

8. People who are condemned love _____ rather than _____. Look at verse 20. What does this mean?

9. The scriptures we have read tell us that people love darkness because they can hide their sin. Jesus is the light and He exposes our sin. Has Jesus exposed the sin in your life to you, allowing you to see your need for salvation? What is your response to this?

10. A friend comes quietly to you one day and asks for an explanation of the gospel. Write what you would tell them.

Let's Pray Together

Dear God, Thank you for the gospel. Thank you that, even after Adam and Eve sinned against you in the garden of Eden, you provided a way of forgiveness to all who would repent of their sin and believe in the Lord Jesus Christ as their Saviour. Thank you for your grace – that undeserved gift which enables us to come to you through Jesus' death on the cross. Thank you that there is nothing that I can do to earn your favour or your forgiveness, but because you are great in mercy and love for us, you have provided forgiveness of sin to all who believe. Help me to understand clearly your gospel that I might receive it, and one day be in eternity with you. Amen

MY ACTION PLAN ...

1.

2.

3.

4.

5.

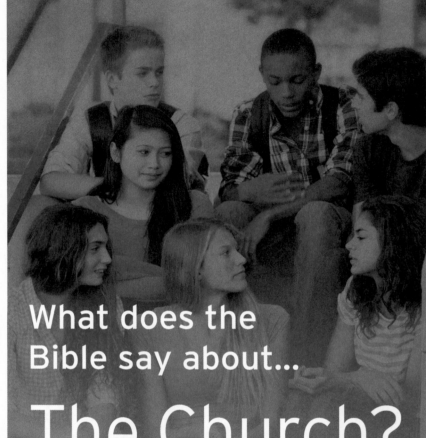

What does the
Bible say about...

The Church?

Think

Ask

Bible

The very first mention of the church came from Jesus' own mouth when He was speaking to Peter. He was speaking with His disciples about who people were saying that He was.

> *[13] Now when Jesus came into the district of Caesarea Philippi, he asked his disciples, "Who do people say that the Son of Man is?" [14] And they said, "Some say John the Baptist, others say Elijah, and others Jeremiah or one of the prophets." [15] He said to them, "But who do you say that I am?" [16] Simon Peter replied, "You are the Christ, the Son of the living God." [17] And Jesus answered him, "Blessed are you, Simon Bar-Jonah! For flesh and blood has not revealed this to you, but my Father who is in heaven. (Matthew 16:13-17)*

Simon Peter had it right! Jesus was the Christ! The Son of the Living God! This is a very significant moment with the disciples because soon afterwards Jesus would go to His death on the cross, leaving the disciples to carry on the work. Finally, Simon Peter got it! God had revealed to him that Jesus wasn't just a prophet, He was the Son of God! Simon's confession of who Jesus is leads on to the very first conversation about the church. And key to any conversation about church is the confession from all who say they are Christians, that Jesus is the Son of God!

> *[15] He said to them, "But who do you say that I am?" [16] Simon Peter replied, "You are the Christ, the Son of the living God." [17] And Jesus answered him, "Blessed are you, Simon Bar-Jonah! For flesh and blood has not revealed this to you, but my Father who is in heaven. [18] And I tell you, you are Peter, and on this rock I will build my church, and the gates of hell shall not prevail against it. (Matthew 16:15-18)*

Here in verse 18 we have the first mention of the word 'church'. But what is Jesus saying? Firstly, Jesus tells Simon that he is blessed, because he understands who Jesus is. This is not from Simon's own wisdom but is revealed to him by God. It's a mark of Simon's true faith.

Did You Know ...?

Jesus is referred to in Scripture as the cornerstone of the church. A cornerstone is a huge rock built into the foundations of a building. Jesus is the foundation of the church. Peter's name means small stone. Jesus, the foundation rock, used Peter, the small stone, to build his church. Note even the power of Satan would or could stop Jesus. Wow!

Jesus also spoke of the church as 'His' church. That means that the church is His. It was paid for by His own blood and death. How does that work? The church is made up of those people (Christians) who are saved through the forgiveness of sin that comes only from the death of Jesus. This means that those who are saved are His. The church is not the building where people gather for worship. The church is God's people whom He has saved and who gather to worship Him.

So, what happened after this conversation between Peter and Jesus? Well, soon after, Jesus was crucified and rose again. He spent some time with His disciples encouraging them to spread the gospel to all the world. He then returned to His Father in heaven. And so begins the early church. We read more about the early church in the book of Acts in the New Testament.

Did You Know ...?

An apostle is someone who is sent with divine authority. Jesus' twelve disciples were all apostles because he gave them the great commission to go into the world to preach the gospel.

In New Testament times God by His Spirit did great miracles through the apostles and gave signs to show that He was working in a new way among the Israelites (Jews) and the Gentiles (everyone else).

Throughout this time, the Apostles role was to preach the gospel and lead this new group of believers, now called the church. What did this early church focus on?

> [42] And they devoted themselves to the apostles' teaching and to fellowship, to the breaking of bread and the prayers. (Acts 2:42)

This was a very hard time for the church, because many people thought these Christians had abandoned the true faith and were following a false religion. The Christians did not do things as they used to in the temple with the priests and religious leaders of the day.

The religious leaders were also feeling threatened because the new way that God wanted the church to function no longer included them. This revealed that they were not serving God but themselves. Throughout Jesus' time on earth He had been confronting the religious leaders with their sin, telling them they needed to repent and obey God not man – but they resented Jesus because He was exposing their selfish hearts. They came up with the plan to have Him killed, but He rose again and provided the way to eternal life. Now Jesus' church was growing in number and leading people away from all the crazy rules that the religious leaders had burdened them with.

Christians came under terrible persecution for their faith. Satan was trying to destroy God's people – but remember what Jesus said to Simon Peter? Not even the power of Satan will stop the Lord from building His church.

So, what then is the church?

The church is not a building. There is such a thing as a church building which we call 'church', but the church that the Bible is speaking of means the group of Christians who gather to worship God. There is the worldwide church, which speaks of all Christians from every nation. There is the local church, which refers to the gathering of a group of Christians in one place. The local church I belong to is called 'River City Bible Church'. We gather every Sunday to worship the Lord and be taught from His Word. We don't have an actual church building to meet in, instead we use a local school hall. But we are still a church.

The Bible also calls the church 'the body of Christ.' This doesn't mean we are Christ's actual physical body, but it does mean that we are a part of His family here on earth, and that we are His spiritual body. Every Christian is part of 'the body of Christ' and each one has a role to play in the church, in caring for one another, praying for one another, and serving one another in the ways that God has gifted us. God has made us all different with different talents and gifts but we are all equally useful to the church.

> [14] For the body does not consist of one member but many. [15] If the foot should say, "Because I am not a hand, I do not belong to the body … [16] And if the ear should say, "Because I am not an eye, I do not belong to the body," that would not make it any less a part of the body. [17] If the whole body were an eye, where would be the sense of hearing? …[18] But as it is, God arranged the members in the body, each one of them, as he chose. [19] If all were a single member, where would the body be? As it is, there are many parts, yet one body. …[27] Now you are the body of Christ and individually members of it. (1 Corinthians 12:14-20, 27)

But Wait, there's More!

What other Principles can we Learn from Scripture?

Bible

The Bible tells us that there are some key things the church should be doing and our earlier verse in Acts is a good place to start.

> *42 And they devoted themselves to the apostles teaching and the fellowship, to the breaking of bread and the prayers. (Acts 2:42)*

We can see four things here that the early church did that lay the foundation for all churches throughout history and today.

1. Teaching

This is the teaching of the Bible. The Apostle Paul said to his young friend, Pastor Timothy, "Preach the Word; be ready in season and out of season; reprove, rebuke, and exhort with complete patience and teaching" (2 Timothy 4:2). The Bible is God's revelation of Himself to Christians and it is what God uses in our lives to grow us, correct us, train us, equip us, and comfort us as we come to know more of Him through His Word. A key part of teaching is the teaching of the gospel – the good news of Jesus, who saves people from their sins.

> *16Let the Word of Christ dwell in you richly, teaching and admonishing one another in all wisdom, singing psalms and hymns and spiritual songs, with thankfulness in your hearts to God. (Colossians 3:16)*

2. Fellowship

Fellowship means that Christians have a common bond together which gives us unity with one another. That unity means that we can

▼ *more...*

encourage one another, build one another up and work together as the Lord would have us do. It does not just mean being together but rather allowing the common bond of Christ to guide our time together. We can worship together, pray together, serve alongside one another, help one another, listen to one another, encourage one another – these are all examples of fellowship.

3. The Breaking of Bread – also known as the Lord's Supper

The bread and the wine are symbolic of Jesus' body and blood. His body which was nailed to the cross and His blood that was shed as payment for our sin. It's a time of reflection to ensure that we have confessed any sin, and to think on the gift that Christ has given us, through His death and resurrection, which is new life in Him!

Communion is also known as the Lord's Supper because the bread and wine were the final meal Jesus shared with His disciples before His crucifixion.

> *19 And he took bread, and when he had given thanks, he broke it and gave it to them, saying, "This is my body, which is given for you. Do this in remembrance of me." 20 And likewise the cup after they had eaten. (Luke 22:19-20a)*

4. Prayer

Prayer is when we speak to God. We can pray by ourselves or with others, but there should always be a time of prayer in church when God's people gather together, because it is God who we worship. When we come together as a church there is something very special about praying together, being of one mind together, as we lift our concerns, our burdens, our worship and our thanks to God.

▼ *more...*

17Pray without ceasing. (1 Thessalonians 5:17)

This verse doesn't mean that we pray every second of every day, but it does mean that we are to be in an attitude of prayer, regularly going to the Lord with the thoughts of our hearts, praying for others and ourselves. This verse shows us that God considers prayer to be very important.

So teaching, fellowship, breaking of bread and prayer, are the foundation or the building blocks of the church. They are the essentials from which other things flow. Each church will look a little different to the next in what else it will be involved in. There might be ministries which reach out to homeless people or single parents, Bible classes for kids at the school down the road, prison ministries, hospital visitation, counselling, missions work overseas, just to name a few. However, central to every true church is the foundation of the gospel – the good news that Jesus came to earth as God's Son. He paid the price for our sins by dying on the cross. On the third day, He rose again, defeating death and providing forgiveness and eternal life for all who confess their sin, and believe in Him. Any church which does not proclaim this good news is not a true church. So now you have a basic history of the church and the important things to look for in a true Bible teaching church.

What Did We Learn about the Church?

• The first mention of church was from Jesus after Peter confessed that Jesus is the Son of God.

• Every church must be built on the confession of the people that Jesus is the Son of God.

• Jesus is the Cornerstone (the Foundation) of the church.

• The church belongs to Jesus and He will build it His way.

• Jesus uses people in the church according to the way He has gifted them to serve one another.

• The church is God's body of people, both around the world and locally too.

• There are four essential things that the church must do. It must teach the Word of God (the Bible), it must gather regularly for fellowship, it must take the Lord's supper regularly, and it must be prayerful. And it must be built on the foundation of the gospel – God's good news of salvation for all who would believe.

Study Questions

[15]He [Christ] is the image of the invisible God, the firstborn of all creation. [16]For by him all things were created, in heaven and on earth, visible and invisible whether thrones or dominions or rulers or authorities – all things were created through him and for him. [17]And he is before all things, and in him all things hold together. [18]And he is the head of the body, the church. He is the beginning, the firstborn from the dead, that in everything he might be preeminent. (Colossians 1:15-18)

1. What do these verses tell us about the church? (who was it created by, and who was it created for?)

2. Christ is the creator of the church. If Christ has created all things, should anything else other than Christ be worshipped? - why/why not?

3. Only God is to be worshipped, not only at church but in every aspect of our lives. What word is used for the worship of a false god?

4. Idolatry is the worship of something other than God. If anything or anyone other than God is worshipped, does that give Jesus pre-eminence (first place)? Give a reason for your answer.

5. Who can be a part of Christ's church?

Let's Pray Together

Dear God, thank you for the church. Thank you for the work you did through the nation of Israel. Thank you that from this nation came your Son who would be the Saviour of all who would repent of their sin and believe in Him as Lord. Thank you that Jesus is the head of your church. I pray that you would grow your church throughout the world and may you be honoured and glorified by your church. Amen.

MY ACTION PLAN ...

1.

2.

3.

4.

5.

What does the
Bible Say about...

Spirit-Filled
Living?

Think

Ask

Bible

Spirit-filled living? What does that even mean? And who does it apply to? These are good questions and ones that we will come to shortly. First, let's go back a step and start from the beginning. What (or, more rightly, 'Who') is the Spirit? The word Spirit refers to the Holy Spirit, the third person of the Trinity. What can we see of the Holy Spirit in the Bible?

Did You Know ...?

The Trinity is the three persons of God. God the Father, God the Son and God the Holy Spirit.

- **The Holy Spirit is Eternal**

The first time we encounter the Spirit of God in the Bible is in fact right at the very beginning.

> *[1] In the beginning, God created the heavens and the earth. [2] The earth was without form and void, and darkness was over the face of the deep. And the Spirit of God was hovering over the face of the waters. (Genesis 1:1-2)*

The Spirit of God is eternal; He has always been and will always be.

> *[14] how much more will the blood of Christ, who through the eternal Spirit offered himself without blemish to God, purify our conscience from dead works to serve the living God. (Hebrews 9:14)*

- **The Holy Spirit Enables God's People**

Through the Old Testament we see many references to the Holy Spirit, often referring to Him as being the One who enables victory and power.

*¹⁰ The Spirit of the L*ORD *was upon him, and he judged Israel. He went out to war, and the L*ORD *gave Cushan-rishathaim king of Mesopotamia into his hand. And his hand prevailed over Cushan-rishathaim. ¹¹ So the land had rest forty years. Then Othniel the son of Kenaz died. (Judges 3:10-11)*

- ## The Holy Spirit Transforms Lives

We also see the Holy Spirit as the one who brings about change in people's lives. When a sinner repents before God, and receives Jesus Christ as their Saviour, they are saved. That work which has happened to make a sinful heart into a humble heart is done by the Holy Spirit. This work He does is called 'regeneration'. It means He takes an old 'dead' (spiritually dead) life, and makes it a new life in Christ!

³ For we ourselves were once foolish, disobedient, led astray, slaves to various passions and pleasures, passing our days in malice and envy, hated by others and hating one another. ⁴ But when the goodness and loving kindness of God our Saviour appeared, ⁵ he saved us, not because of works done by us in righteousness, but according to his own mercy, by the washing of regeneration and renewal of the Holy Spirit. (Titus 3:3-5)

- ## The Holy Spirit Enables Miracles

³⁰ And the angel said to her, "Do not be afraid, Mary, for you have found favour with God. ³¹ And behold, you will conceive in your womb and bear a son, and you shall call his name Jesus. ³² He will be great and will be called the Son of the Most High. And the Lord God will give to him the throne of his father David, ³³ and he will reign over the house of Jacob forever, and of his kingdom there will be no end." ³⁴ And Mary

> *said to the angel, "How will this be, since I am a virgin?"* [35] *And the angel answered her, "The Holy Spirit will come upon you, and the power of the Most High will overshadow you; therefore the child to be born will be called holy—the Son of God.* [36] *And behold, your relative Elizabeth in her old age has also conceived a son, and this is the sixth month with her who was called barren.* [37] *For nothing will be impossible with God." (Luke 1:30-37)*

Wow! The angel had visited with Mary to tell her that she was going to have a baby – a special baby, a divine baby – and that he was going to be in her womb because the Holy Spirit would put him there. Can you imagine that!

- **The Holy Spirit is also called 'Comforter' or 'Helper'**

The Holy Spirit is called 'the Comforter' (John 14:16) which means 'one called alongside to help'. When Jesus was on earth He was the counsellor and help for His disciples. Now all Christians are Jesus' disciples and so he has left us the Holy Spirit to be our counsellor, opening our eyes to understand God's Word, giving us strength and help for this life which can sometimes be confusing and tough. He will never leave us.

- **The Holy Spirit is the author of the Bible**

> [21] *For no prophecy was ever produced by the will of man, but men spoke from God as they were carried along by the Holy Spirit. (2 Peter 1:21)*

This verse tells us that it was not man's doing to write the Bible, but the Holy Spirit working in and through the human authors to give His words.

- **The Holy Spirit and Jesus**

But what about when Jesus the baby grew to be Jesus the man? Was the Holy Spirit still needed? Did He still perform miracles and change hearts and enable victory to God's people? Yes, the Holy Spirit was at work even when Jesus walked this earth, and as we read through the New Testament, we see more and more of the work of the Holy Spirit.

The Holy Spirit came down on Jesus at His baptism, giving Him power to preach the good news of salvation, teaching the disciples, healing and performing miracles.

> [21] Now when all the people were baptized, and when Jesus also had been baptized and was praying, the heavens were opened, [22] and the Holy Spirit descended on him in bodily form, like a dove; and a voice came from heaven, "You are my beloved Son; with you I am well pleased." (Luke 3:21-22)

> [37] … you yourselves know what happened throughout all Judea, beginning from Galilee after the baptism that John proclaimed: [38] how God anointed Jesus of Nazareth with the Holy Spirit and with power. He went about doing good and healing all who were oppressed by the devil, for God was with him. (Acts 10:37-38)

Even after Jesus went to His death on the cross, death was not victorious! Why? Because three days after Jesus' death, the Holy Spirit raised Jesus from the dead. That's just a small glimpse of who the Holy Spirit is and what He does. We haven't talked about what 'Spirit-filled living' means yet, so keep reading!

But Wait, there's More!

What other Principles can we Learn from Scripture?

Bible

> *¹¹ If the Spirit of him who raised Jesus from the dead dwells in you, he who raised Christ Jesus from the dead will also give life to your mortal bodies through his Spirit who dwells in you. (Romans 8:11)*

Let me start by telling you what 'Spirit-filled living' doesn't mean. It doesn't mean that we need to keep looking for ways to get the Holy Spirit. Whenever someone becomes a Christian, the Holy Spirit comes to live inside of them.

> *¹⁶ Do you not know that you are God's temple and that God's Spirit dwells in you? (1 Corinthians 3:16)*

This means that He works within us, helping us to turn away from sin and enabling us to live a life which honours God. He also comforts us, opening our eyes to understand the Bible, convicting us of sin, and helping us to be obedient to God. Once a person becomes a Christian, he/she can't lose the Holy Spirit. He will live inside of them always (Romans 8:9). It also means that once a person has the Holy Spirit, He will be at work in their lives too. That's what Galatians 5:22 refers to when the Apostle Paul speaks of the fruit of the Spirit in our lives – love, joy, peace, patience, kindness, goodness, gentleness, self-control. These things are easily seen in Christians because of the Holy Spirit at work in them.

> *¹⁵ Look carefully then how you walk, not as unwise but as wise, ¹⁶ making the best use of the time, because the days are*

▼ *more...*

evil.[17] Therefore do not be foolish, but understand what the will of the Lord is. [18] And do not get drunk with wine, for that is debauchery, but be filled with the Spirit, [19] addressing one another in psalms and hymns and spiritual songs, singing and making melody to the Lord with your heart,[20] giving thanks always and for everything to God the Father in the name of our Lord Jesus Christ, [21] submitting to one another out of reverence for Christ. (Ephesians 5:15-21)

Look back at the verses in Ephesians 5. The Apostle Paul is describing how a believer must live. A Christian should…

- **Walk Wisely (v.15)**

He reminds the Ephesian church that they are to be wise in how they conduct their day to day lives. We already know that true wisdom comes only from God and His Word, not according to the world.

- **Make the Best use of Time (v.16)**

In other words, don't waste your time on things which are not good for you. What we spend our time on is a good indication of what the priorities of our lives are. Are we using our time in the best way?

- **Understand God's Will for your Life (v.17)**

Remember, God's will for your life is not a mystery that we cannot know. God's will for us is to be saved, to live our life in obedience to Him, to daily confess our sins and to choose to live according to the truths of Scripture. Outside of that, we have free will to choose a job, hobbies, the college we attend – remembering that all of these decisions will be influenced by our desire to love God above all.

▼ *more…*

- **Avoid getting Drunk (v.18a)**

You might wonder what this has to do with you if you are not in the habit of drinking alcohol. Look at it this way. When someone is drunk, they are no longer in control of themselves. Their actions, words, attitudes and abilities are under the influence of the alcohol. This scripture is telling us not to put ourselves under the influence of alcohol, or anything else! It could apply to drugs, hypnotism and witchcraft, the world's philosophy – all these things require you to give up control over your own mind and body. Instead place yourself under the control of the Holy Spirit by being dependent on Him to teach you more of God through the Bible, to convict your heart of sin, and to continue to change you according to God's mercy in your life.

- **The Outward Signs of the Spirit's work in you (vv. 19-20)**

The Bible says that we are to address "one another in psalms and hymns and spiritual songs, singing and making melody to the Lord with your heart,giving thanks always and for everything to God the Father in the name of our Lord Jesus Christ." We are to gather to sing praises to the Lord, to hear Scripture being read, and to give thanks to God for all that He has done for us. We can do this in church, as a family around the dinner table, as well as in our Bible Study groups.

- **Submit to Authorities in your Life (v. 21)**

God has placed rightful authorities over each one of us. Parents, church leaders, teachers – each have a God given role to help you, and in response you are to respect and humbly submit yourself to them. Why do this? Because it shows your reverence for Jesus.

▼ *more...*

- **The Fruit of the Spirit**

> ²²But the fruit of the Spirit is love, joy, peace, patience, kindness, goodness, faithfulness, ²³gentleness, self-control; against such things there is no law. (Galatians 5:22-23)

I mentioned earlier that the Apostle Paul speaks of the work of the Holy Spirit in the lives of Christians which we know as 'the fruit of the Spirit'. I remember as a child in Sunday School, the teacher giving us paper cut outs of fruit and we needed to write the fruit of the Spirit on them. It was a fun way to learn this verse and also it meant I had something to stick to my mirror at home to see every day and remind me every day. These nine character traits or attitudes are what the Holy Spirit is at work to achieve in each one of us. They are 'markers' or things that outwardly identify genuine believers. While unbelieving people still reflect these things in their lives to some degree because they are made in the image of God, only the believer has the ability to produce these things in a way that pleases God, because they have the Spirit dwelling within them and producing fruit. These character traits in our lives are not the result of us working hard to earn salvation. They are not a way of trying to manipulate people into liking us, nor are they something that we use to deceive people about what's really going on in our hearts. They are the work of the Spirit in transformed hearts. They give God glory. It's never about how wonderful we are because of how loving we are, or how much self-control we show, or how kind we are towards others. It's the opposite. It's about how wonderful God is because of the amazing work that He has done in the heart of a sinner which now reflects glory to Him.

▼ more...

What if we mess up and some days we are unkind to our siblings, or lacking in joy, or are not gentle in our manner with people? Does that mean that we have lost the Holy Spirit? No. The Holy Spirit will never leave a true believer. But even believers are still sinners. We will still sin, and may even sin often. But the difference is that a Christian is saved from the consequence of their sin. Christ has paid the penalty on our behalf and we are no longer under the power of sin. Until we go to heaven, we will always be prone to sin. But when we sin we can come straight to Jesus for His forgiveness, and move on. And as we grow in our Christian faith, the Holy Spirit's enabling power in our lives will mean that we are more able to turn from temptation. When we are saved, we will not instantly become a shining example of the fruit of the Spirit. But over time, the Spirit will grow us in each of these characteristics and it will become more obvious in our lives that changes are happening in these areas.

Spirit-filled living. It's not as mysterious as it sounds is it? In fact it's pretty neat. Having the Spirit in our lives begins that wonderful transformation of becoming more and more like Jesus!

What did we Learn about Spirit-filled living?

• The Holy Spirit is the third person of the Trinity – God in three persons. We learnt some things about the Holy Spirit:

- The Holy Spirit is Eternal

- The Holy Spirit Enables God's People

- The Holy Spirit Transforms Lives

▼ *more...*

- The Holy Spirit Enables Miracles

- The Holy Spirit is also called 'Comforter' or 'Helper'

Ask

- The Holy Spirit is the author of the Bible

- The Holy Spirit empowered Jesus

- The Holy Spirit raised Jesus from the dead

- The Holy Spirit lives inside of (indwells) every Christian

- The Holy Spirit will never leave Christians

• Spirit-filled living means living under the control and influence of the Holy Spirit

• Christians do not need to look for any further 'filling' or experience of the Holy Spirit

• The fruit of the Spirit is love, joy, peace, patience, kindness, goodness, faithfulness, gentleness and self-control: these things should become more and more obvious in the lives of Christians as they grow in their faith.

Study Questions

¹⁵"If you love me, you will keep my commandments. ¹⁶ And I will ask the Father, and he will give you another Helper, to be with you forever,¹⁷ even the Spirit of truth, whom the world cannot receive, because it neither sees him nor knows him. You know him, for he dwells with you and will be in you.

¹⁸ "I will not leave you as orphans; I will come to you. ¹⁹ Yet a little while and the world will see me no more, but you will see me. Because I live, you also will live. ²⁰ In that day you will know that I am in my Father, and you in me, and I in you. ²¹ Whoever has my commandments and keeps them, he it is who loves me. And he who loves me will be loved by my Father, and I will love him and manifest myself to him." ²² Judas (not Iscariot) said to him, "Lord, how is it that you will manifest yourself to us, and not to the world?" ²³ Jesus answered him, "If anyone loves me, he will keep my word, and my Father will love him, and we will come to him and make our home with him. ²⁴ Whoever does not love me does not keep my words. And the word that you hear is not mine but the Father's who sent me. ²⁵ "These things I have spoken to you while I am still with you. ²⁶ But the Helper, the Holy Spirit, whom the Father will send in my name, he will teach you all things and bring to your remembrance all that I have said to you. ²⁷ Peace I leave with you; my peace I give to you. Not as the world gives do I give to you. Let not your hearts be troubled, neither let them be afraid. (John 14:15-27)

1. Finish these sentences from the first two sentences (vv. 15-17) above. Those who love Jesus will... Jesus asked the Father for the Holy Spirit for... The other name Jesus used for the Holy Spirit is... The Holy Spirit will be with believers... The world cannot receive the Holy Spirit because...

2. Jesus calls the Holy Spirit 'the Spirit of Truth'. What do you think that this means?

3. Spirit of Truth means that it is only the Holy Spirit who can communicate truth to us because it comes from Him. What do you think this means we should do if there are parts of the Bible that we don't understand, or that we find hard to obey?

4. When Jesus told the disciples that He would not leave them as orphans, He was referring to His upcoming death and return to His Father in Heaven. What did He mean when He said He would not leave them as orphans?

5. Jesus spoke of many wonderful things to the disciples, but He was soon to leave them. They perhaps felt worried they would forget what He had taught them. What else did Jesus say which would comfort them over this worry?

6. These words of Jesus to His disciples also have some application to us. What three things about the Holy Spirit can we know from these verses?

Let's Pray Together

Dear God, Thank you for what we have learnt about your Holy Spirit. Thank you for sending Him as a helper and comforter to us. Thank you that He lives inside every believer, and that He helps us to understand and live by your Word. There is so much about the Holy Spirit that we have learnt. Thank you for providing us with the help that we need so that you would be glorified. Amen.

But the fruit of the Spirit is love, joy, peace, patience, kindness, goodness, faithfulness, gentleness, self-control; against such things there is no law. Galatians 5:22-23

MY ACTION PLAN ...

1.

2.

3.

4.

5.

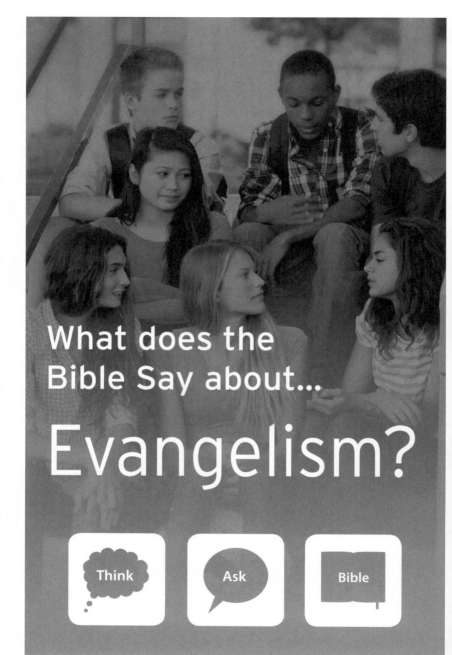

Imagine this if you can. There was this guy called Jonah and his full time job was to proclaim the Word of the Lord. He was a prophet. Initially he proclaimed the Word just to his own people, the Israelites, until God told Jonah to go and evangelise the Ninevite people who needed to be saved from their sin.

Did You Know ...?

Evangelism is the sharing of the gospel - the good news that God promises salvation to all who repent of their sin and believe in him. They are to follow him all their days.

But Jonah refused. He hated the Ninevites. They were sworn enemies of Israel. Instead, he purchased a one-way ticket on a ship heading in the other direction, and off he went. Did he, a prophet, really think that he could flee from the presence of God? The Bible tells us that no one can.

> *7 Where shall I go from your Spirit?*
>
> *Or where shall I flee from your presence?*
>
> *8 If I ascend to heaven, you are there!*
>
> *If I make my bed in Sheol, you are there!*
>
> *9 If I take the wings of the morning*
>
> *and dwell in the uttermost parts of the sea,*
>
> *10 even there your hand shall lead me,*
>
> *and your right hand shall hold me.*
>
> *(Psalm 139:7-10)*

During the voyage the winds blew and the waves began to rage and crash and throw the ship about. Even the sea-hardened sailors feared for their lives and they each cried out to their gods. But Jonah knew what was happening. He knew that God's hand of discipline was at work to bring him to repentance. So instead of repenting, he told the sailors to throw him into the depths of the sea, and they would all be saved. Even now, it seems Jonah is trying to escape God, thinking to drown himself. Eventually, the sailors reluctantly did as Jonah instructed, and the storm calmed immediately. If you think that is crazy, then what happens next is quite extraordinary.

> *17And the LORD appointed a great fish to swallow up Jonah. And Jonah was in the belly of the fish three days and three nights. (Jonah 1:17)*

God did not allow Jonah to end his life by drowning, instead He sent a huge fish to swallow Jonah for three days and nights. During those days and nights, Jonah repented of his disobedience. Then the fish vomited him up on land and Jonah went on to Nineveh where he told them of judgement to come.

> *4Jonah began to go into the city, going a day's journey. And he called out, "Yet forty days, and Nineveh shall be overthrown!" 5 And the people of Nineveh believed God. They called for a fast and put on sackcloth, from the greatest of them to the least of them.*

> *6The word reached the king of Nineveh, and he arose from his throne, removed his robe, covered himself with sackcloth, and sat in ashes.7 And he issued a proclamation and published through Nineveh, "By the decree of the king and his nobles: Let neither man nor beast, herd nor flock, taste anything. Let them not feed or drink water, 8 but let man and beast be covered with sackcloth, and let them call out mightily to God. Let everyone turn from his evil way and from the violence*

that is in his hands. ⁹ Who knows? God may turn and relent
and turn from his fierce anger, so that we may not perish." ¹⁰
When God saw what they did, how they turned from their evil
way, God relented of the disaster that he had said he would
do to them, and he did not do it. (Jonah 3:4-10)

When I read this account, my heart leaps for joy at the thought of an entire city and its authorities turning to God. Jonah should have been beside himself with excitement! Imagine, all of those people saved from the penalty of their sin! Except, Jonah wasn't happy. He was angry. He did not want God to offer salvation to the wicked Ninevites. He wanted to keep it for the Israelites only. Jonah was exceedingly selfish. The hope of evangelism is to see men and women, and boys and girls hear the Word of God, believe it and repent of their sin and have faith in God's forgiveness. But this was not Jonah's desire. He obeyed the Lord in going to Nineveh to preach but he did not long for the people's salvation. How terribly sad. We don't know the end of the story, of what happened to Jonah. Did he come to see the wickedness of his heart? His lack of love for those who are unsaved? His arrogance to disagree with God? I hope so.

Even though Jonah's story is a very sad one, we can learn some valuable lessons about evangelism from it. We'll also look at some other verses which tell us a similar lesson from Scripture.

1.   God loves all people and even though their wickedness is offensive to God, His desire is that they would be saved. Jonah sadly showed a lack of love towards the people of Nineveh, and he was terribly wrong. God's desire is that we love all people and be obedient to take the Word of God to them.

¹ Now the word of the LORD came to Jonah the son of Amittai,
saying,² "Arise, go to Nineveh, that great city, and call out
against it, for their evil has come up before me." (Jonah 1:1-2)

> *³ This is good, and it is pleasing in the sight of God our Saviour, ⁴ who desires all people to be saved and to come to the knowledge of the truth. (1 Timothy 2:3-4)*

2.   God is Sovereign over the salvation of people. Despite their wickedness, if God opens their eyes to their need for Him, they will respond.

> *³ So Jonah arose and went to Nineveh, according to the word of the LORD. Now Nineveh was an exceedingly great city, three days' journey in breadth. ⁴ Jonah began to go into the city, going a day's journey. And he called out, "Yet forty days, and Nineveh shall be overthrown!"⁵ And the people of Nineveh believed God. They called for a fast and put on sackcloth, from the greatest of them to the least of them. Jonah 3:3-5 ⁶⁵ And he said, "This is why I told you that no one can come to me unless it is granted him by the Father." (John 6:65)*

DID YOU KNOW? WHEN JONAH FINALLY OBEYED GOD AND WENT TO NINEVEH, 120,000 PEOPLE WERE SAVED!

3.   God uses His people to spread the gospel to the whole world. Our responsibility is to go, and share the gospel with all those who do not believe, regardless of our own personal desires or opinions.

> *² "Arise, go to Nineveh, that great city, and call out against it, for their evil has come up before me." (Jonah 1:2a)*

> *¹⁹ Go therefore and make disciples of all nations, baptizing them in the name of the Father and of the Son and of the Holy Spirit, ²⁰ teaching them to observe all that I have commanded you. And behold, I am with you always, to the end of the age." (Matthew 28:19-20)*

4.   God saves all who call out to Him in repentance. Jonah's attitude or even our own fearful or poor attempt to share the gospel is no barrier to God saving a person from their sin.

> [10] When God saw what they did, how they turned from their evil way, God relented of the disaster that he had said he would do to them, and he did not do it. (Jonah 3:10)

> [17] When the righteous cry for help, the LORD hears and delivers them out of all their troubles.(Psalm 34:17)

But Wait there's More!

What other Principles can we Learn from Scripture?

Bible

> [18] And Jesus came and said to them, "All authority in heaven and on earth has been given to me. [19] Go therefore and make disciples of all nations, baptizing them in the name of the Father and of the Son and of the Holy Spirit, [20] teaching them to observe all that I have commanded you. And behold, I am with you always, to the end of the age." (Matthew 28:18-20)

These verses are from a portion of scripture known as 'The Great Commission'. Matthew records that Jesus has been raised from the dead after His crucifixion and is now among the believers once again. His eleven remaining disciples had gathered to worship Him and these are the words that He spoke to them. The first thing He says is that He is the ultimate authority in heaven and on earth. His Father had given Him that authority. And because of that, He commanded the believers to go and make disciples. How were they to do that? By sharing the gospel

▼ more...

– the very gospel that they had the privilege to witness and receive themselves. This command is not only intended for the disciples. It's also for us. Jesus commands all of us to go and share the gospel. But there is one thing that is very important for us to consider before we go and share the gospel. We must make sure we know the gospel ourselves. Let's have a look at that together.

- We must understand God is holy. There is none holy like the Lord. (1 Samuel 2:2a, 1 John 1:5)

When we say that God is holy, we mean that He is without sin. God is pure and separate from anything evil. God created us to enjoy a friendship with Him where we grow to know Him, and respond to Him by loving, worshipping and obeying Him as the centre of our lives.

- We must understand that we are all sinners. *For all have sinned and fall short of the glory of God. (Romans 3:23)*

Sadly, we are unable to enjoy this friendship with God because of sin. Sin is anything that displeases God or fails to meet His standards. In order for us to be right with God, we need to be righteous people. Righteous means perfect in the eyes of God, but the Bible says that no one is like this; everyone has sinned. Sin not only separates us from God, but it also makes us God's enemies rather than His friends. Unless we can have our sins forgiven, we will never be able to be friends with God and we will never have eternal life with Him. We are, instead, in danger of receiving God's punishment for our sins and there is nothing we can do to earn God's forgiveness.

- We must understand that forgiveness requires a sacrifice. *Without the shedding of blood there is no forgiveness of sins. (Hebrews 9:22b)*

▼ *more...*

To receive God's forgiveness in the old days, God required people to bring a perfect lamb or goat to the priests at the temple. The animal would be sacrificed (which showed that the animal was being punished instead of the person) and the sinner would then be forgiven by God. God also promised that one day He would provide a greater sacrifice which would take away sin once and for all. This sacrifice would be Jesus, God's one and only Son.

- We must understand that Jesus came to pay the price for our sin. *Behold, the Lamb of God, who takes away the sin of the world! (John 1:29)*

God sent Jesus, His only precious and perfect Son, to die in our place and take the punishment that we deserve. He was born as a baby in Bethlehem, grew up in a family in the land of Israel, and at the age of about thirty began a special mission to carry out His Father's plan to rescue sinners. This meant that He would later be mistreated and suffer a cruel death by being nailed to a cross of wood, even though He had done nothing wrong. However, God raised Jesus from the dead on the third day and, now, because of Jesus' sacrifice, God offers forgiveness and the invitation to know Him.

- We must understand that we need to receive God's offer of forgiveness.

> [16]*For God so loved the world, that he gave his only Son, that whoever believes in him should not perish but have eternal life. (John 3:16)*

To receive God's gift of forgiveness and come into a right relationship with Him, we must:

▼ *more...*

ADMIT that we have sinned against God and be willing to turn away from our sins (repent).

BELIEVE that Jesus is the Son of God; that He is fully God fully human, and that He paid the penalty for our sins when He died on the cross, and that He rose again from the dead.

FOLLOW the Lord Jesus in your life. He gives you the strength to live for Him each day. So…. the big question is: have you received the good news of the gospel for salvation for yourself? Have you prayed to God admitting your sin and turning from it, telling Him you believe in His Son as the payment for your sins, and committing to follow Jesus all your days in His strength?

If you have, Matthew 28:19-20 is for you. "Go therefore and make disciples of all nations, baptizing them in the name of the Father and of the Son and of the Holy Spirit, teaching them to observe all that I have commanded you. And behold, I am with you always, to the end of the age."

What did we learn about Evangelism?

- God loves all people and desires that all people would be saved.

- God is sovereign over salvation.

- God uses Christians to share the gospel.

- God saves all those who cry out to Him in repentance and faith.

- It is the responsibility of all Christians to share the gospel with unbelievers.

- We must make sure we know and believe the gospel ourselves before we can share it.

Study Questions

⁶I am astonished that you are so quickly deserting him who called you in the grace of Christ and are turning to a different gospel— ⁷ not that there is another one, but there are some who trouble you and want to distort the gospel of Christ. ⁸ But even if we or an angel from heaven should preach to you a gospel contrary to the one we preached to you,let him be accursed. ⁹ As we have said before, so now I say again: If anyone is preaching to you a gospel contrary to the one you received, let him be accursed. (Galatians 1:6-9)

The above verses are taken from a letter that the Apostle Paul wrote to the Galatian church. In my Bible, the title above this section of scripture reads; 'No other Gospel'. That's what these verses are about. Paul is warning the Galatian church that there is no other gospel than the true, saving gospel of Jesus Christ. It seems a shame that Paul should have to warn the people about this, but when we consider it, it makes sense. Satan has been trying to destroy God's people from the beginning when he chose to rebel against God, and one of the ways he does this is to deceive people with a false gospel.

1. There are two types of gospel. There is the true gospel of Jesus Christ, and there are false gospels. The true gospel tells us that salvation comes through Jesus Christ, through His death on the cross which pays for the sins of those who believe in Him. A false gospel will deny salvation is through Jesus' death, but tells people that they can somehow earn forgiveness or favour from God. What word does Paul use in verse 7 to describe what people 'do' to the gospel?

2. The word 'distort' means to change the form or the meaning of something. What does Paul say will happen to anyone who distorts the gospel of Jesus?

3. The word 'accursed' in verse 9 means to come under eternal judgement. It is the most serious judgement anyone could face. Why do you think that to proclaim a false gospel brings such serious consequences?

4. What verses from this chapter could you memorise to help you in sharing the true Gospel with those who need to hear it? Why don't you spend some time writing out those verses on cards so you can put them somewhere where you will see them often.

Let's Pray Together

Dear God, Thank you for the gospel of Jesus Christ. It is the good news that not only tells us that we are sinners, but also tells us how we can be saved through the forgiveness of our sins through Jesus' death on the cross. Thank you that you loved us so much that you sent Jesus to pay for our sin so that we wouldn't have to. Thank you that there is nothing that we can do or even need to do to earn your forgiveness or favour – Jesus has done it all. Please protect us from the lies of a false gospel. May we stand firm in truth. Please will you help us to go and share the gospel with those who do not believe. It seems scary sometimes to do that, but please give us courage and wisdom. Amen.

MY ACTION PLAN ...

1.

2.

3.

4.

5.

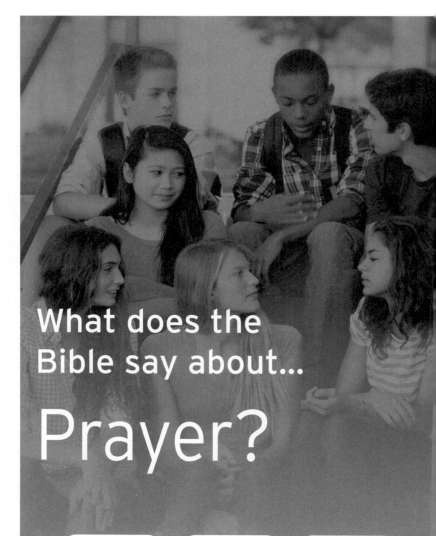

What does the
Bible say about...

Prayer?

Think

Ask

Bible

A man had a daily practice that he refused to give up. Every day, three times a day, he would go to his room, kneel before the open windows and pray to God. This had been important to him for most of his life – he was probably around eighty years-old at this time. He had an important job, overseeing the king's governors. He had seen a lot of life and had served under at least three kings. But one day a trap was set, and this man willingly and knowingly walked right into it. Let's go back a step….

Did You Know ...?

When the law forbids something which God has commanded, Christians must obey God.

As I said, the man had a very important role in the kingdom, and because of his excellent reputation the king was about to promote him over the whole kingdom. What an incredible opportunity! But there were men who didn't want this man in that role. Perhaps there were men who worked in the king's court who were jealous of him. Maybe they were stealing from the king and they knew that with this guy in charge, they wouldn't get away with it any longer. Whatever their reason, they had to get rid of him – they just needed a plan. It was pretty easy really. They knew that this man was a worshipper of God and that he knelt at the window of his room to pray, three times a day. So, these wicked men appealed to the king's pride by suggesting that anyone who prayed to someone other than the king should be thrown into the den of lions.

Hey – wait a minute! Den of lions? So, this old man is… Daniel? Yep! Are you surprised? Maybe you thought this happened to Daniel when he was a young man? But the Bible tells us that he is not young when he meets the lions face to face. He began serving under the reign of

Nebuchadnezzar as a young man, but that was three kings ago, and Daniel is still hard at work serving, now under King Darius. And it seems Darius was as prideful as Nebuchadnezzar.

> [1] *"It pleased Darius to set over the kingdom 120 satraps, to be throughout the whole kingdom;* [2] *and over them three high officials, of whom Daniel was one, to whom these satraps should give account, so that the king might suffer no loss.* [3] *Then this Daniel became distinguished above all the other high officials and satraps, because an excellent spirit was in him. And the king planned to set him over the whole kingdom.* [4] *Then the high officials and the satraps sought to find a ground for complaint against Daniel with regard to the kingdom, but they could find no ground for complaint or any fault, because he was faithful, and no error or fault was found in him.* [5] *Then these men said, "We shall not find any ground for complaint against this Daniel unless we find it in connection with the law of his God."*
>
> [6] *Then these high officials and satraps came by agreement to the king and said to him, "O King Darius, live forever!* [7] *All the high officials of the kingdom, the prefects and the satraps, the counsellors and the governors are agreed that the king should establish an ordinance and enforce an injunction, that whoever makes petition to any god or man for thirty days, except to you, O king, shall be cast into the den of lions.* [8] *Now, O king, establish the injunction and sign the document, so that it cannot be changed, according to the law of the Medes and the Persians, which cannot be revoked."* [9] *Therefore King Darius signed the document and injunction.* (Daniel 6:1-9)

Now we all know that Daniel ignores this crazy order from the king. In fact…

> When Daniel knew that the document had been signed, he went to his house where he had windows in his upper chamber open towards Jerusalem. He got down on his knees three times a day and prayed and gave thanks before his God, as he had done previously. (Daniel 6:10)

Daniel was not going to be told by mere men (even by a mere king, because after all he served the King of Kings!) that he could not pray for thirty days. We've read already, prayer was Daniel's regular practice.

Even though Daniel knows his life is on the line, he chooses to disobey the king's order and instead continues to pray as he normally did. We might wonder why Daniel did not shut the windows and pray in secret so he could not be caught. The Bible does not tell us what his reasons were in responding this way to the king's order. But it does tell us that on finding out about this terrible order not to pray, Daniel knew he needed to pray. Not just because he needed rescuing from these men who were out to destroy him, but because prayer was Daniel's spiritual lifeline. Remember that Daniel was not 'a local'. He had been exiled (kidnapped!) from his home in Jerusalem many years earlier and forced to work in the king's household. Instead of doing all he could to escape and get home, Daniel did all he could to honour God in whatever he was doing. God was faithful to Daniel and caused him to be looked favourably upon by those in charge of him, until eventually he worked his way up through the ranks of the king's servants. Now, the foreigner is suddenly about to be in charge of the locals. None of this is random, nor is it just luck. Daniel was being used by God in this foreign land, and knew his need for God's help. How did he get that help? He went to God in prayer, depending on God's wisdom, strength and help.

Interestingly, we don't read that Daniel goes to his room and cries out to God for help. No, we read that he goes to his room and gives thanks to God – as he has done previously. Daniel knew he had much to thank God for. He knew that God was in control and that whatever happened was in God's hands. Even in a time of horrific trial – Daniel surely knew he was going to be thrown to the lions – he got down on his knees to give thanks.

Another Bible writer tells us to also have that same attitude.

> [16] *Rejoice always,* [17] *pray without ceasing,* [18] *give thanks in all circumstances; for this is the will of God in Christ Jesus for you. (1 Thessalonians 5:16-18)*

These verses were written by the Apostle Paul to the church in Thessalonica where they were experiencing persecution. He wants to encourage the people there to continue on in their faith, even amidst trials and difficulties, reminding them to be joyful and prayerful. Paul and Daniel were obviously of the same mind in knowing that prayer needs to be frequent. Prayer isn't a one-off conversation each Sunday, or a quick 'thanks for dinner' each evening. Imagine if you were to only speak with your dearest friend like that! But God is the dearest of all friends to those who believe in Him, and we are to talk regularly with him. Paul's encouragement to 'pray without ceasing' does not mean that we are to pray twenty-four hours a day. That would be impossible! But like Daniel, we are to pray often throughout the day. We don't have to make specific times for when we pray – although that might be helpful. Neither are we limited to praying just in one certain place – like Daniel in front of his window, although it might be helpful to have a place to go to when we pray. The idea is that we make prayer a regular and protected time during our day. Paul, like Daniel, also speaks of giving thanks to Jesus when we pray. Why? Because it's God's will for us to be thankful. When we are thankful, we remember that whatever is happening is all in God's hands because He is totally in control – we can be very thankful for that!

So, we know that the Bible says prayer is to be a regular part of our lives, and that we are to gives thanks when we pray. Is that it?

But wait there's more!

What other principles can we learn from Scripture?

Yes, we are to pray often, and we are to be thankful in our prayers – but what else? Is there a way that we should pray? Things that we should ask for? Let's see what Jesus says.

> *⁵ "And when you pray, you must not be like the hypocrites. For they love to stand and pray in the synagogues and at the street corners, that they may be seen by others. Truly, I say to you, they have received their reward. ⁶ But when you pray, go to your room and shut the door and pray to your Father who is in secret. And your Father who sees in secret will reward you. ⁷ "And when you pray, do no heap up empty phrases as the Gentiles do, for they think that they will be heard for their many words. ⁸ Do not be like them, for your Father knows what you need before you ask him." (Matthew 6:5-8)*

The first thing Jesus does is warn us against being hypocrites. The word hypocrite means 'actor'. He says we are not to be like those who love to stand out in public and pray loudly so that others will see and hear and think how very well we can pray, or how spiritual we sound. Look below at an example of someone who did just that.

> *¹⁰ "Two men went up into the temple to pray, one a Pharisee and the other a tax collector. ¹¹ The Pharisee, standing by himself, prayed thus: 'God, I thank you that I am not like*

▼ *more...*

other men, extortioners, unjust, adulterers, or even like this tax collector. [12] I fast twice a week; I gives tithes of all that I get.' [13] But the tax collector, standing far off, would not even lift up his eyes to heaven, but beat his breast, saying, 'God, be merciful to me, a sinner!' [14] I tell you, this man went down to his house justified, rather than the other. For every one who exalts himself will be humbled, but the one who humbles himself will be exalted." (Luke 18:10-14)

In this parable (an earthly story with a heavenly meaning), Jesus compares two men. One was a Pharisee and he believed that he was righteous because of his good works and behaviour. The other was a tax collector who knew that there was nothing that he could do to earn God's forgiveness, and instead cried out in humility and distress. What did Jesus say about them? The tax collector went home as a man saved from his sin. The Pharisee did not. But what does this have to do with prayer? The prayers of these men revealed their hearts. The Pharisee was full of pride and believed he was better than anyone else. He felt that he did not need God for anything, because he believed he had done it all for himself. Sadly, his prayer revealed that he did not serve God – but instead he served his own pride. The tax collector, however, was a broken man. He did not draw attention to himself, and he cried out to God for forgiveness. His prayer was genuine, not just a performance for everyone to see. God answered his prayer. Jesus finishes the parable by reminding us to be humble before God – or God will humble us. Make sure that your prayer is not an act, making you look good before others, or even tickling your own pride. Humble yourself before God as you pray.

▼ *more...*

What else do we see in the verses in Matthew? Jesus tells us to go somewhere private to pray. It protects our hearts from the temptation to want to make ourselves look good in front of others. It also allows us to quieten our hearts and minds before the Lord, allowing us to come with respect and awe of Him. Does that mean we cannot pray anywhere except our bedroom? No, remember Jesus prayed in the garden! We can pray anywhere, but the principle is that it is helpful to have somewhere private and quiet, away from the eyes and ears of others.

Jesus also tells us not to 'heap up empty phrases as the Gentiles do, for they think they will be heard for their many words'. The Gentiles must have had a wonderful vocabulary of big important sounding words and phrases – but we don't need that. We are to come with our normal language, knowing that God will hear us. Think about the tax collector, all he said was "God, be merciful to me, a sinner." That's pretty simple isn't it? And God not only heard, but answered his prayer. Jesus reminds us that God knows what we need before we even ask for it. Does that mean we don't need to ask Him? No, it just means we don't need to try and explain everything to God, as if He isn't aware of what is happening in our lives. He knows, He cares and He is just waiting for us to ask for our needs.

Jesus also had some words for us on what we should pray for. This is not a rigid list to follow when we pray, but a model of what we should base our prayers on.

> [9] *Pray then like this. "Our Father in heaven, hallowed be your name.* [10] *Your kingdom come, Your will be done, on earth as it is in heaven.* [11] *Give us this day our daily bread,* [12] *and forgive us*

▼ *more...*

> *our debts, as we also have forgiven our debtors. [13] And lead us*
> *not into temptation, but deliver us from evil. (Matthew 6:9-13)*

Let's look at the word 'hallowed'. It means 'holy' or 'sacred'. When we pray we are to remember this about God, and acknowledge it before Him. Not only does that honour God but it reminds us of the attitude in which we are to approach God. An attitude of humility.

Second, whatever we are praying about, we must make sure that God's will is the most important thing to us. Sometimes when we pray it's easy for us to submit a shopping list of requests – even for good things. But we always need to remember that God's will is more important than our own.

Third, it is right to ask God for what we need. And don't forget to be thankful for His daily provisions for us.

Fourth, we must make sure that we regularly confess any sin to God, asking His forgiveness.

And lastly, we need to remember to ask God for His protection from anything which might hurt us spiritually.

What did we Learn about Prayer?

- Prayer is a very important part of our relationship with God.

- Prayer is to be a regular part of our lives.

- We need to be thankful when we pray.

- We are not to be a hypocrite in our prayers, but to be genuine.

- We are to guard our hearts against the pride of wanting others to think well of us for our prayer.

- We are to pray remembering that God is holy.

- We are to pray desiring God's will above our own desires.

- We are to come to God asking for what we need.

- We are to confess our sin to God.

- We are to ask God for His protection and help.

Study Questions

> *⁹ And it is my prayer that your love may abound more and more, with knowledge and all discernment, ¹⁰ so that you may approve what is excellent, and so be pure and blameless for the day of Christ, ¹¹ filled with the fruit of righteousness that comes through Jesus Christ, to the glory and praise of God. (Philippians 1:9-11)*

This prayer is one of the Apostle Paul's, written to the believers in the Philippian church.

1. What is Paul praying for in verse 9?

2. Paul is praying that the people's love would be Biblical; grounded firmly in the truths of God's Word and commands. Verse 10 tells us why this is important – write this out in your own words.

3. Paul's prayer is that the people would grow in their ability to love. Often we pray for the needs that we can see – perhaps someone is unwell or travelling, or they are going through hard times. It is good to pray for these things, but it's also good to follow Paul's example and pray for 'heart issues' – that people would grow to love others as the Bible teaches us to love. The reason Paul prays for these things is so that God would be praised and glorified. Do you pray things for people so that God can be praised and glorified? Why or why not?

4. How can you use Paul's prayer as an example to follow? What things could you pray for your family or friends? Choose someone you love, and write a prayer for them.

5. What is your prayer routine? Do you pray each day? Do you make a list of what to pray for? Do you just pray if you need God's help?

6. What have you learnt today that you will put into practice this week?

Let's Pray Together

Dear God, Thank you that we can come to you anytime, anywhere and talk to you. Thank you that you listen to us and that we can share the burdens, the joys, the praise and the confessions of our hearts. Thank you for Daniel's example to us of prayer – he was a man who knew that he needed to speak regularly with you, to gain your peace, your comfort, your strength and your wisdom for the important job you had for him. Thank you that even though he must have been frightened at the thought of being thrown to the lions, you enabled him to be strong and courageous and that he honoured you above all. Please help us to pray, as Daniel did, regularly with praise and thanksgiving, not wanting to impress anyone, but having a genuine and respectful awe of you. You are a holy God and we are so blessed to be able to come to you in prayer. Please forgive us for the times we turn from you and neglect to come to you. Help us to make prayer a regular and necessary part of our day. Amen.

Rejoice always, pray without ceasing, give thanks in all circumstances; for this is the will of God in Christ Jesus for you.
1 Thessalonians 5:16-18

MY ACTION PLAN ...

1.

2.

3.

4.

5.

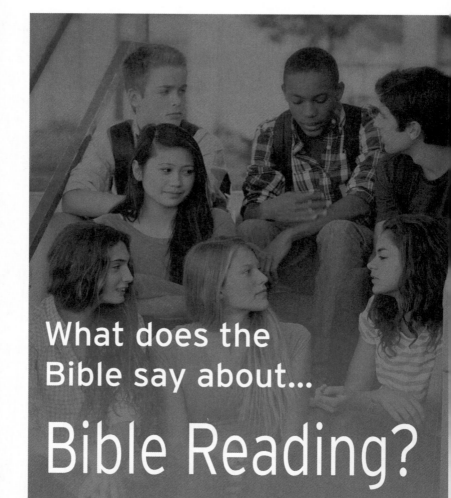

What does the
Bible say about...

Bible Reading?

Think

Ask

Bible

When I was in Sunday School we were challenged to memorise Psalm 1. It's also the first passage of Scripture that my husband memorised as a boy. We both still remember it exactly as we learnt it – and I can even remember standing in front of the church to recite it, before being handed a beautifully wrapped prize!

> [1]*Blessed is the man*
>> *who walks not in the counsel of the wicked,*
> *nor stands in the way of sinners,*
>> *nor sits in the seat of scoffers;*
> [2]*but his delight is in the law of the LORD,*
>> *and on his law he meditates day and night.*
> [3]*He is like a tree*
>> *planted by streams of water*
> *that yields its fruit in its season,*
>> *and its leaf does not wither.*
> *In all that he does, he prospers.*
> *(Psalm 1:1-3)*

But why is Psalm 1 so important? Well, it's not that it's any more important than any other passage in the Bible, but it does tell us some very important things. Let's look together at what the first part of Psalm one says.

It begins by telling us that there is someone who is blessed. The word blessed means 'happy'. Let's try that word in the sentence.

> *"Happy is the man who walks not in the counsel of the wicked, nor stands in the way of sinners, not sits in the seat of scoffers; but his delight is in the law of the Lord, and on his law he meditates day and night." (Psalm 1:1-2)*

The person is only blessed when they don't live as sinners do because they delight in the law of the Lord, and meditate on it day and night.

Did You Know ...?

Seven days of Bible reading makes one week, but seven days without Bible reading makes one weak! Get it?

What does that mean?

'The law of the Lord' is the first five books of the Bible (also called 'the Pentateuch'). We believe they were written by Moses. The person who wrote Psalm 1 would not have had the whole Bible, but they would have had those books of the law which they knew were given to them by God. Those who loved God treasured the law of the Lord. Why?

The first five books of the Bible are a record of the history of Israel. Genesis starts with the beginnings of the world and tells us about the creation of the earth and all that is in it, including the first man and woman. It tells us about the fall of man into sin and their removal from the presence of God – but it also tells us of God's rescue plan for mankind, through the provision of His Precious Son. We read of the expansion of mankind throughout the world, the different languages and cultures, the people who honoured God and those who did not. We read of God's continual forgiveness of His people, the Israelites, and their continual falling back into sin, their crying out to Him for forgiveness, and again, their falling into sin – highlighting to us the truth that God is quick to forgive, and patient and longsuffering with His people. We see Satan's ongoing efforts to destroy God's people, the ways in which God thwarts those plans, and the ways in which God is glorified. We see the shocking sin of mankind resulting in God sending a worldwide flood and saving only eight people, and then the re-establishment of humanity on earth once more. We read of slavery and freedom, and we see the amazing miracles of God versus the evil power of Satan. There is a massive exodus of millions of people who were once captive, now freed but wandering in the desert, their sin and their grumblings causing God to discipline them over and over.

We see God's faithfulness in the provision of a land which overflowed with milk and honey, the victories over kings and countries and possession of lands for their families. We read the laws given to guide people to walk in the ways of the Lord, and we see the wisdom of God in showing man that He cannot save himself by his own good works. Every so often we see glimpses of Jesus, the One who was to come as The Lamb who would take away the sin of the world. No wonder the Israelite people treasured this law. They understood it to be the inspired Word of God.

> *16All Scripture is breathed out by God and profitable for teaching, for reproof, for correction, and for training in righteousness, 17that the man of God may be complete, equipped for every good work. (2 Timothy 3:16-17)*

In these verses above, the Apostle Paul reminds young pastor Timothy that all Scripture is inspired by God. Isn't verse 16 wonderfully worded? 'All Scripture is breathed out by God…' It gives us a picture of God literally breathing out all that the Bible contains. While the words were written on paper by men chosen by God, the actual words used came from God.

No wonder the Psalmist (the person who wrote Psalm 1) says that the man who delights in the law of the Lord is blessed! But the next thing he says is very interesting.

> *2 but his delight is in the law of the LORD, and on his law he meditates day and night. Psalm 1:2*

Not only does this blessed man (or woman, boy or girl) delight in the law of the Lord but he/she meditates on it day and night. Meditation is a word that we hear quite a lot today and it can have different meanings. The Biblical meaning of meditation means to allow your mind to dwell/think on Scripture.

> [16]*Let the word of Christ dwell in you richly, teaching and admonishing one another in all wisdom, singing psalms and hymns and spiritual songs, with thankfulness in your hearts to God. (Colossians 3:16)*

The Word of Christ is to dwell in us richly. How is that to happen? We are to read the Word regularly, giving ourselves time to think on it, study its meaning, memorise it and apply it to our lives. But what do we see from Psalm 1, for the person who meditates on the law of the Lord?

> *He is like a tree planted by streams of water that yields its fruit in its season, and its leaf does not wither. In all that he does, he prospers. (Psalm 1:3)*

Scripture paints a picture for us of a tree that is thriving by the stream. Its roots are deep in the soil and have ready access to all the water it needs for its survival. A tree that is healthy and thriving where it is planted will produce fruit each season. Its leaves will be healthy, any fruit it produces will be beautiful and good to taste. That's a description of the person who doesn't walk in the way of the wicked but instead meditates on the Word of God, allowing it to dig deep into the soil of their heart. They will thrive spiritually. They will grow and produce spiritual fruit.

The Apostle Paul lists for us in his letter to the Galatian church what the spiritual fruit is that we should be seeing in our lives if we are thriving. But the Psalmist describes, at the end of Psalm 1, the wicked.

> ⁴ *The wicked are not so,*
>
> *but are like chaff that the wind drives away.*
>
> ⁵ *Therefore the wicked will not stand in the judgment,*
>
> *nor sinners in the congregation of the righteous;*
>
> ⁶ *for the LORD knows the way of the righteous,*
>
> *but the way of the wicked will perish.*
>
> *(Psalm 1:4-6)*

The wicked (those who are not Christians) will not thrive. Outwardly it might look like they are – their lives might seem great. But these things are temporary. God is concerned more with the condition of our hearts. The description of the wicked is that they are like chaff that the wind blows away. Do you know what 'chaff' is? It is the outside husk of the corn or the seed. It's useless. In the days when this Psalm was written, the harvest would be gathered in the fields and stripped of the outside husk which the wind would then pick up and whisk away. This is not saying that unbelievers do not have skills or usefulness in society. But sadly, that usefulness cannot save a sinful heart when it comes time for them to stand before God at their death.

There is much in this life that we can chase, or that we can set our affections on. This Psalm calls us to remember that whatever we set our affections on needs to have an eternal significance. And it tells us that the Word of God is what brings that eternal significance to our lives. It is what tells us of our sinful standing before a holy God. It shows us that there is nothing that we can do to redeem ourselves in the eyes of God. And then it shows us Jesus. He is the Saviour of those who will humble themselves and come to Him. The Bible is life to all who read it and respond to it. Blessed is the one who meditates on the law of the Lord. Do you?

But wait there's more!

What other principles can we learn from Scripture?

We've seen from Psalm 1 why meditating on and reading the Bible is so important, but perhaps you are wondering just how to do it? And what happens when you come to a part that you don't understand? Maybe you have always thought that the Bible was written for old people? Well, let's start right there. What does the Bible say about it only being written for old people?

12 Let no one despise you for your youth, but set the believers an example in speech, in conduct, in love, in faith, in purity. (1 Timothy 4:12)

Again, we have the words of the Apostle Paul, writing to encourage his young friend Timothy. He is not only writing to Timothy - the Bible is for all of us. He is writing to encourage you too. As Christian young people, you are to set an example for other believers in your speech, your conduct, your love, faith and purity. How do you know what God expects of you in these things? You find it in the Word of God – which as we saw in Psalm 1, brings spiritual fruit like those mentioned in 1 Timothy 4:12, to those who dwell richly in its pages everyday.

You are never too young to read, memorise, study and apply the Word of God. So let's look together at how to read the Word of God and meditate on it.

- Pray

    18Open my eyes, that I may behold wondrous things out of your law. (Psalm 119:18)

It's always good to pray before we read the Bible, asking God's help to understand it, to see more of Him in it, and to be changed by it.

▼ *more...*

- Read

> [9] *How can a young man keep his way pure? By guarding it according to your word.* [10] *With my whole heart I seek you; let me not wander from your commandments!* [11] *I have stored up your word in my heart, that I might not sin against you.* (Psalm 119:9-11)

These verses from Psalm 119 remind us of what Psalm 1 has already told us. For young people to keep their ways pure, they need the Word of God stored up in their hearts. Here's some ideas how to do that.

1. Reading plans.

There are many reading plans available which will guide you on what to read each day, with a goal in mind – such as reading through the Bible in one year. These can be great, but you might find it moves too fast through the Bible without giving you much help in understanding the parts you find tricky.

2. Devotional books

There are many devotional books written to encourage young people to read their Bibles and apply it to their lives. You could ask your pastor or another adult to recommend one for you. Another good way to find one would be to look at the website of this publisher who have many helpful devotional books (www.christianfocus.com)

3. Study Bibles

There is a type of Bible called a study Bible which on every page has study notes which help us to understand more.

▼ more...

4. Commentaries

Commentaries are not just for adults. A commentary is a book written to give an accurate interpretation of the Bible. Again, the publisher of this book has many commentaries which might be useful to you. Ask a Christian adult like your parents or pastor, if you would like to read one.

Whatever method or resource you use, you want to make sure the Bible has the significant role. Don't just read a devotional book without opening your Bible. Don't just read study notes or a commentary without opening your Bible and reading it for yourself. And always approach your time reading God's Word with a heart that is focused and ready. I find it helpful to pray before I read my Bible – to ask God firstly to forgive any sin which might get in the way of a rich time in the Word, and then to ask Him to open my eyes to see more of Him, to learn more of His ways, and to understand things which might be difficult. Remember, the Christian who reads their Bible has the Holy Spirit living inside them, helping them to understand, to apply and to grow.

- Meditate

> *⁸ This Book of the Law shall not depart from your mouth, but you shall meditate on it day and night, so that you may be careful to do according to all that is written in it. For then you will make your way prosperous, and then you will have good success. (Joshua 1:8)*

Why is it so important to meditate on the Word of God? The verses above tell us that it's so we can be careful to obey it. When we

▼ *more...*

meditate (think about) Scripture, we take the opportunity to study and understand it so that we can remember it and obey it. There are different ways to do this. Some people keep a journal of the Scriptures they have read, any observations they have made about the verses, other scriptures that come to mind which say a similar thing, and some ways in which they can apply it to their life. This is a great way to meditate on Scripture. Others like to use books or study guides which ask questions about the verses, giving them an opportunity to write down their answers. The idea is not to burden yourself with a big homework task of Scripture study, but rather to be able to read and learn from God's Word so that you can apply it to your life. You might try a few different ideas to help you find the way that is best for you to read and think about God's Word.

- Memorise

> [11] *I have stored up your word in my heart, that I might not sin against you. (Psalm 119:11)*

What does it mean to store up God's Word in our hearts? It means to think on it so you can use it for another time. When we do this God's Word can protect us. When we are tempted to sin it is there as a reminder to obey God instead. It can become a comfort for us when we are tired or frightened. It can become an encouragement for someone to hear God's Word when they share their troubles with us. It can remind us of the character and awesomeness of God when we are in the middle of a field, looking up at the stars on a dark night. There have been all sorts of times when Scripture, which is hidden in my heart, has helped me. Let me encourage you to work on your memorisation of Scripture too.

▼ *more...*

What did we Learn about Bible Reading?

1. The Bible is God's Word, written by God for us. We need to read it so we can know God, know about ourselves, and know what God's plan is for us.

2. Those who read God's Word will be blessed if they follow it and apply it to their lives.

3. God uses His Word the Bible to produce spiritual fruit in our lives, making us more like Him.

4. We are never too young to be reading and studying the Bible.

5. It's good to pray before we read the Bible, asking God to help us understand His Word.

6. There are many resources available to us to help us in our Bible reading time. But we need to ensure that the Bible is the priority of our time.

7. Meditating on Scripture helps us to understand it, and to apply it to our lives.

8. Memorising Scripture 'stores it up' in our hearts.

Study Questions

> [7]*The law of the* Lord *is perfect, reviving the soul; the testimony of the* Lord *is sure, making wise the simple;* [8] *the precepts of the* Lord *are right, rejoicing the heart; the commandment of the* Lord *is pure, enlightening the eyes;* [9] *the fear of the* Lord *is clean, enduring forever; the rules of the* Lord *are true, and righteous altogether.* [10] *More to be desired are they than gold, even much fine gold; sweeter also than honey and drippings of the honeycomb.* [11]*Moreover, by them is your servant warned; in keeping them there is great reward. (Psalm 19:7-11)*

1. Psalm 19:7-11 uses four different words to describe God's Word to us. What are they?

2. Verses 7-9 use six different phrases which describe what God's Word does for us. What are they?

3. Choose one of these phrases above, and give an example of this in your own life.

4. Verse 10 uses a precious and valuable metal to compare with God's Word. Why would it do that?

5. Why would verse 10 say that God's Word is more valuable than gold, or sweeter than honey? What is this verse saying to us?

6. Verse 11 tells us that God's people are warned by God's Word. What is it that we are warned about? How does it warn us?

7. The second part of verse 11 speaks of great reward for those who obey God's Word. What would this great reward be? Can you think of any other Scripture which would support your answer?

Let's Pray Together

Dear God, Thank you for your Word the Bible. Thank you that you have breathed it out and that it is life for all who will read it and obey it. Thank you that it is wisdom for us, and that it is what you use in our lives to teach us of yourself, to show us more of ourselves, and to change us and grow us. Please help us to make reading your Word a priority in our lives. Please help us to meditate and think on it, to understand it, to store it up in our hearts, and to be able to apply it to our lives. Amen.

MY ACTION PLAN ...

1.

2.

3.

4.

5.

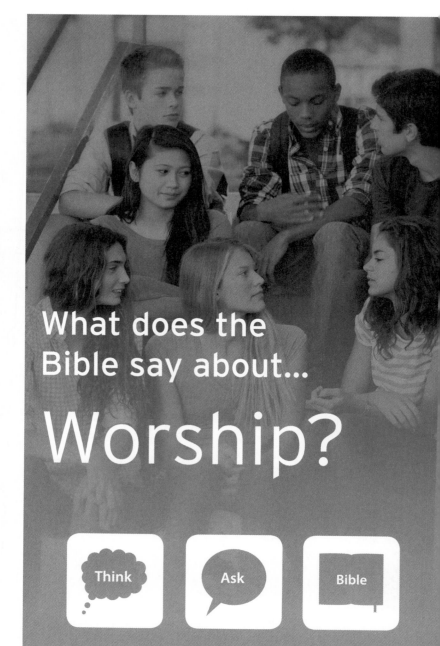

What does the
Bible say about...

Worship?

Think

Ask

Bible

We are all worshippers. It's true. In fact, we were created to worship. The problem though, is that many people are worshipping the wrong thing.

> [1]And God spoke all these words, saying, [2]"I am the LORD your God, who brought you out of the land of Egypt, out of the house of slavery. [3] "You shall have no other gods before me. [4x]"You shall not make for yourself a carved image, or any likeness of anything that is in heaven above, or that is in the earth beneath, or that is in the water under the earth. [5] You shall not bow down to them or serve them, for I the LORD your God am a jealous God, visiting the iniquity of the fathers on the children to the third and the fourth generation of those who hate me, [6] but showing steadfast love to thousands of those who love me and keep my commandments. (Exodus 20:1-6)

You might recognise these verses of Scripture above as coming from the Ten Commandments. God gave these commandments during the time when He had enabled the Israelites to make their escape from slavery to the Egyptians after over 200 years, and now they were in the desert. It was time for God to remind the Israelites of their responsibilities to Him, their God. Think about it, these Israelites had been born and raised in Egypt where they were surrounded by a culture which worshipped many gods. God was reminding the Israelites that He alone was God, and that they were to worship no other gods.

Did You Know ...?

Worship is the feeling or expression of reverence and adoration.

But what happened next? Moses went up Mt Sinai to receive instruction from the Lord, and he took longer than the people thought he should.

> *¹When the people saw that Moses delayed to come down from the mountain, the people gathered themselves together to Aaron and said to him, "Up, make us gods who shall go before us. As for this Moses, the man who brought us up out of the land of Egypt, we do not know what has become of him." ²So Aaron said to them, "Take off the rings of gold that are in the ears of your wives, your sons, and your daughters, and bring them to me."³ So all the people took off the rings of gold that were in their ears and brought them to Aaron. ⁴And he received the gold from their hand and fashioned it with a graving tool and made a golden calf. And they said, "These are your gods, O Israel, who brought you up out of the land of Egypt!" ⁵When Aaron saw this, he built an altar before it. And Aaron made a proclamation and said, "Tomorrow shall be a feast to the Lord." ⁶And they rose up early the next day and offered burnt offerings and brought peace offerings. And the people sat down to eat and drink and rose up to play. (Exodus 32:2-6)*

Aaron was Moses' brother. He was with Moses back in Egypt when Moses approached Pharaoh, and now he was Moses' right hand man in the desert. Or so Moses thought.

Aaron had been influenced by Egyptian culture. The calf was one of many idols worshipped throughout Egypt. What happened next? The Israelites proclaimed the golden calf to have brought them out of Israel! Aaron built an altar and they tried to mix the worship of an idol made by man with worship of the True and Living God.

What was it that God had said to them earlier?

> *And God spoke all these words, saying, ² "I am the Lord your God, who brought you out of the land of Egypt, out of the house of slavery. ³ "You shall have no other gods before me.*

> [4] *"You shall not make for yourself a carved image, or any likeness of anything that is in heaven above, or that is in the earth beneath, or that is in the water under the earth.* [5] *You shall not bow down to them or serve them, for I the LORD your God am a jealous God, visiting the iniquity of the fathers on the children to the third and the fourth generation of those who hate me. (Exodus 20:1-5)*

What a mess. God told Moses what was happening in camp, and sent him back to the people. Of course Moses was furious. So was God. And why wouldn't He be? The Israelites had cried out to Him in slavery from Egypt and He had freed them, promising them a wonderful new life. But at the first chance they had, they changed teams. They chose to worship false gods, made by their own hand. As a result, many of the Israelites died that day. God is a jealous God and He expects His children to obey His commandments.

Years later, after Moses died, God placed Joshua as His servant who would lead the Israelites into the promised land. He was, like Moses, a man who loved God and worshipped Him alone. God spoke to the people again, this time through Joshua, about this issue of who they will worship.

> [14] *"Now therefore fear the LORD and serve him in sincerity and in faithfulness. Put away the gods that your fathers served beyond the River and in Egypt, and serve the LORD.* [15] *And if it is evil in your eyes to serve the LORD, choose this day whom you will serve, whether the gods your fathers served in the region beyond the River, or the gods of the Amorites in whose land you dwell. But as for me and my house, we will serve the LORD."* *(Joshua 24:14-15)*

Do you see what I see in this passage? Choice. God was not making the people worship Him. No, He gave them a choice. He gives you and I choice too. We might not have a golden calf in the living room that we worship, but if we look deep into our hearts, we will see the things that we are tempted to worship. Worship isn't just bowing down before an idol. It's making 'something or someone' a priority in your life. It's often the thing that we think so highly of that if we didn't have it we would be unhappy. It could be friendship, money, popularity with people, the way we look (or want to look), control over others, time on a computer or game, or the dream of something you want for your future. None of these things in themselves are bad, but it's the emphasis or priority that we give them in our lives which show us if we've made idols of them or not. Have a think, just as Joshua was challenging the people, 'choose this day whom you will serve.' And remember, your decision will have eternal consequences.

But wait, there's more!

What other principles can we learn from scripture?

I appeal to you therefore, brothers, by the mercies of God, to present your bodies as a living sacrifice, holy and acceptable to God, which is your spiritual worship. (Romans 12:1)

It would be fair to ask, what exactly does worshipping God look like? Obviously, we can't bow down to Him because we cannot see Him. So how does He want us to worship?

Paul answers the question here for us in his letter to the church in Rome. God wants us to present our bodies as a living sacrifice, holy and acceptable to Him. Does that mean that we literally have to put on our best clothes and somehow present ourselves each day to Him? No. What are the key words in this verse which describe

▼ *more...*

worship? The first word I see is 'present' – you could use the word 'dedicate' in the same way. We have to present/dedicate ourselves to God – firstly in the form of confessing our sin and coming to Christ for salvation. Then it's an ongoing acknowledgment that our lives belong to Him now.

> [20] *I have been crucified with Christ. It is no longer I who live,*
> *but Christ who lives in me. And the life I now live in the flesh*
> *I live by faith in the Son of God, who loved me and gave*
> *himself for me. (Galatians 2:20)*

These verses, also written by the Apostle Paul in a letter to the Galatian church, describe what our life is once we become a Christian. We haven't literally been crucified with Christ, but we are identified with Christ when we repent of our sin and turn to Jesus for salvation; we chose to turn from (or die to) our old life – so we move from being independent from Jesus to dependant on Him for life. When we become a Christian, the Holy Spirit comes and lives within us, guiding us and helping us to be more like Christ in all we think, believe, say and do. Paul finishes by saying that the life a Christian now lives is lived by faith – meaning that it's a life of obedience to Christ, who died so that we might have life.

When we live in a way that acknowledges that our lives belong to Jesus, we live in a way which honours Him. It might be easy to think that this is all about 'doing'. That worship is all about our activities for God. It's not. It all starts with our hearts. Think back to the Pharisees in the time of Jesus. We saw a lot of what they did, didn't we. But was Jesus pleased with their service or works for Him?

> [9] *He also told this parable to some who trusted in themselves*
> *that they were righteous, and treated others with contempt:*

▼ more...

> [10] *"Two men went up into the temple to pray, one a Pharisee and the other a tax collector.*[11] *The Pharisee, standing by himself, prayed thus: 'God, I thank you that I am not like other men, extortioners, unjust, adulterers, or even like this tax collector.* [12] *I fast twice a week; I give tithes of all that I get.'*[13] *But the tax collector, standing far off, would not even lift up his eyes to heaven, but beat his breast, saying, 'God, be merciful to me, a sinner!'*[14] *I tell you, this man went down to his house justified, rather than the other. For everyone who exalts himself will be humbled, but the one who humbles himself will be exalted." (Luke 18:9-14)*

In this parable Jesus compares the Pharisee who considered himself honest and right in all he does to a tax collector. Tax collectors in those days had a reputation for being dishonest in taking money from people. The Pharisee was proud of his own works, trusting in his own good living to get him to heaven. But the tax collector saw his need for a Saviour. He understood that he could not save himself from his own sin, and needed God's mercy. It was the tax collector who went home saved, not the Pharisee. Jesus didn't even mention the good works of the Pharisee. Rather, he spoke of humility. When we humble ourselves before God, acknowledging our sin before Him, it is the beginning of a life of worship. When we promote ourselves to others, trying to pretend to be doing it for God, we worship ourselves.

Let's look back at the verse in Romans 12:1. What other words do we see as describing how we should worship God? The next would be 'living sacrifice'. What does that mean? It just means that whatever we do in our bodies, do it for God's glory. Sometimes what we have to do

▼ *more...*

will be hard – like speaking truth when people don't want to hear it. Or being honest or kind to someone who we feel doesn't deserve it. That is sacrificial living. We make a sacrifice in order that God is honoured.

Then the words 'holy' and 'acceptable' are next. Holy means set apart. Often doing the right thing does set us apart from everyone else. That's hard to do if you just want to blend in, isn't it? We might be the one in our group who doesn't watch certain TV programmes, because we know that it's not right to be involved in those things. We are to do whatever is acceptable to God. Why? Romans 12:1 tells us that when we live in this way, this is our spiritual act of worship. Not just a physical act of worship which means that outwardly we do everything that honours God, but a spiritual act of worship which means it flows from a heart attitude of putting God first.

What did we Learn about Worship?

1. We are all worshippers because we were made to worship. But many people choose not to worship the right thing.

2. God created us to worship Him. He is a jealous God who does not want His children to worship anything or anyone else.

3. We cannot mix worship of God with whatever our culture is worshipping.

4. God will not make us worship Him, but our choice will have an eternal consequence.

5. True worship flows from a right heart attitude.

6. Worship means that we make God first in all we do and desire.

7. Worship requires that we are set apart from the world's culture, instead pursuing what honours God.

Study Questions

²³Sing to the LORD all the earth! Tell of his salvation from day to day. ²⁴Declare his glory among the nations, his marvellous works among all the peoples! ²⁵For great is the LORD, and greatly to be praised, and he is to be feared above all gods. ²⁶For all the gods of the peoples are worthless idols, but the LORD made the heavens. ²⁷Splendour and majesty are before him; strength and joy are in his place. ²⁸Ascribe to the LORD, O families of the peoples, ascribe to the LORD glory and strength! ²⁹Ascribe to the LORD the glory due his name; bring an offering and come before him! Worship the LORD in the splendour of holiness; ³⁰tremble before him, all the earth; yes, the world is established; it shall never be moved. ³¹Let the heavens be glad, and let the earth rejoice, and let them say among the nations, "The LORD reigns!" (1 Chronicles 16: 23-31)

Worship is not just 'doing' life with the right attitude. It's acknowledging truth about God, singing His praises, and meditating on who He is. The verses above are an example of worship from the book of 1 Chronicles in the Bible.

1. What three things in verses 23-24 does the writer praise God for?

2. What three words describe how the writer wants to worship God?

3. Why does the writer want to worship God? (vv. 25-26)

4. What four words describe God in verse 27?

5. The word 'ascribe' in verses 28-29 means 'think of'. Why would the writer encourage people to think of God in these ways? How would that lead people to worship?

6. The writer tells people to 'tremble before Him' in verse 30. What attitude do you think people need to have before they can 'tremble' before God? What is it that makes people 'tremble' before God?

7. What does 'The Lord reigns' mean? Could you say, 'The Lord reigns!' in my life? Why or why not? Are there any changes you need to make?

8. Write your own worship response to the Lord.

▼ *more...*

Let's Pray Together

Dear God, Thank you that you have created us to be worshippers. Forgive us for the times when we have not worshipped you, but have set our hearts on something else. Help us to keep you as our focus, to desire to honour you above all because you are the One who deserves all honour and praise. You are the great God who has rescued your people from their sin, and provided for them an eternal inheritance. You are wonderful, kind, compassionate, slow to anger and quick to forgive. Thank you. The Lord reigns! Amen.

MY ACTION PLAN ...

1.

2.

3.

4.

5.

CHRISTIAN FOCUS PUBLICATIONS

Christian Focus   Christian Heritage   CF4K   Mentor

Christian Focus Publications publishes books for adults and children under its four main imprints: Christian Focus, CF4K, Mentor and Christian Heritage. Our books reflect our conviction that God's Word is reliable and Jesus is the way to know him, and live for ever with him.

Our children's publication list includes a Sunday school curriculum that covers pre-school to early teens, and puzzle and activity books. We also publish personal and family devotional titles, biographies and inspirational stories that children will love.

If you are looking for quality Bible teaching for children then we have an excellent range of Bible stories and age-specific theological books.

From pre-school board books to teenage apologetics, we have it covered!

Find us at our web page:
www.christianfocus.com

CF4 •K
Because you're never
too young to know Jesus